MARY MORNING
MARTHA DAY

MARY MORNING MARTHA DAY

A MARY MORNING MAKES FOR A MARTHA DAY

PAM LILLY

DEDICATIONS

This book is dedicated to my beloved mother, Rose, who was my biggest cheerleader. Her dedication and devotion to God was a shining example throughout my life. She is greatly missed. Knowing that she is in the presence of our Lord and Savior Jesus Christ brings me great joy and gives me hope in our eternal future.

∞ ∞ ∞

This book is also dedicated to my dear friend, Elizabeth, who loved me as if I were her own daughter. She poured into me spiritually and freely shared her wisdom with me. I miss my dear friend and rejoice in knowing I will see her again one day in our heavenly home.

∞ ∞ ∞

I also dedicate this book to my dear mother-in-law, Minnie, who gave me the most wonderful gift I've ever been given—my husband—a man who loves me and loves the Lord. I thank her for her Christian values and integrity, which she passed down to those she held dear. She also loved me like a daughter and left an eternal impact on my life.

CONTENTS

INTRODUCTION

Mary and Martha are two of the most prominent women in the Bible. They offer wonderful life lessons for both men and women to draw from at any stage of life. My purpose for writing this book is to encourage and inspire people of all ages, genders, and walks of life to seek the Lord daily and spend time alone with Him. As with any life lesson, the sooner we learn it, the longer it is beneficial to us. We are wise to study the lives of Martha and Mary with two questions in our hearts: What makes them friends of Jesus? What kept Him coming back to their home again and again? He certainly appears to value time at their home, perhaps as a retreat from the ministry work He came into the world to accomplish. As we examine their lives and attributes, we will see how they were successful in attracting Jesus. And we'll benefit from both His correcting them and the insight He gives them when they lose sight of what is most important in the grand scheme of life.

The sisters' combined lives offer us the perfect balance of devotion and service that Jesus is calling each of us to enjoy. In Luke 10:41–42 the Lord tells Martha, "You are worried and upset about many things, but one thing is necessary. Mary has made the right choice, and it will not be taken away from her." If anything will cause you to stop and evaluate what you are doing and how you are spending your time, it is having Jesus Himself identify and expose things that are of less importance. Jesus's observation reshaped

Martha into a more useful vessel. It opened the door to His purpose for her life.

The fact that Jesus repeatedly visits their little village of Bethany throughout the Gospels is evidence that Jesus is enjoying the company of a repurposed and more focused Martha. This wake-up call for Martha also invites us to examine and inspect our lives in search of similar, undesirable traits Martha was prone to exhibit.

Likewise, we can learn from what Mary does right in these passages, which supports our drawing nearer to our Lord. We must examine what Mary did to cause Jesus to speak so favorably of her choice. Mary chose one single habit that changed her life immeasurably for the better. Spending time with God is well worth every effort we make, no matter how long it takes to master this incredibly rewarding discipline. Now before you say, "I have tried that and failed miserably," or "I have tried, and it didn't do all that for me," let me say we are probably not talking about the same thing. It might be that any person commenting in such a way has not yet learned how to relax, renew, and refresh in His presence while drawing on His power, glory, and wisdom to help accomplish His wonderful plan. This distinct discipline of spending time with God sets you up for a successful day of service that is pleasing to God.

A Martha Day is a joyful day of service unto the Lord. You may not be able to discern what I mean by a "Martha Day" just yet, but you will better understand its meaning as we take a closer look at Martha's life. We will combine what is successful about Martha's life and Jesus's commendations of what makes Mary's life even more successful and marry the two together. Doing so will allow us to come away with an understanding of what it means to be a servant of Jesus Christ, who is pleasing to God and deserving of those coveted words from the Master, "Well done good and faithful servant."

"His master said to him, 'Well done, good and faithful servant! You were faithful over a few things; I will put you in charge of many things. Share your master's joy'" (Matt. 25:21 KJV).

1

PARALLEL LIVES

∞ ∞ ∞

Martha, Mary, and Lazarus's importance to Jesus is evidenced by the fact that they are mentioned in all four Gospels. The apostle John notes in his Gospel, "Now Jesus loved Martha, her sister, and Lazarus" (John 11:5). Both Luke and John recount the story of a particular jaunt into Bethany by Jesus and the disciples. On this extraordinary day Martha was probably serving Jesus and His disciples for the first time. She is introduced, by name, in the Gospel of Luke.

While they were traveling, He entered a village, and a woman named Martha welcomed Him into her home. She had a sister named Mary, who also sat at the Lord's feet and was listening to what He said. But Martha was distracted by her many tasks, and she came up and asked, "Lord, don't You care that my sister has left me to serve alone? So tell her to give me a hand." The Lord answered her, "Martha,

1

Martha, you are worried and upset about many things, but one thing is necessary. Mary has made the right choice, and it will not be taken away from her." (Luke 10:38–42)

Now, I am not a preacher or a theologian, but I am a Martha, sharing many of her traits and tendencies. I understand her desire for everything to be perfect for the most honored guest to grace any home. Being a follower of Jesus for more than forty years, I've heard many sermons and teachings from this passage of Scripture. In many instances Martha gets a bad rap for her response to the pressure brought on by this impromptu "Jesus and Disciples Dinner." I suspect this is probably why the story is included in our Bibles at all—not because Mary was doing the right thing by listening while at the feet of Jesus but because Martha urges Jesus to rebuke Mary for what she considered doing nothing. Luke 10:40 demonstrates a frustrated Martha, "Lord, don't You care that my sister has left me to serve alone? So tell her to give me a hand."

The first thing I comprehend about this great teaching story is that Martha, apparently, had no foreknowledge of Jesus' visit. She appears to have spontaneously welcomed the Master and all of His friends into her home. That tells me a lot about Martha. Here is a woman whose house was consistently presentable, welcoming, and ready to receive guests. Martha was both comfortable with and capable of entertaining larger groups at a moment's notice. The text does not explicitly say Martha served food. It simply says, "But

Martha was distracted with much serving." This statement leads us to assume she planned to serve a meal.

Martha doesn't seem to think twice about having this impromptu dinner party. This act exemplifies the readiness of her servant's heart. She must have mentally calculated the amount of work she had just taken on in one breath. What she couldn't foresee was the behavior of her sister Mary, who had undoubtedly pitched in and helped on prior occasions. How could she have guessed her sibling would be mesmerized by Jesus's words and, therefore, be no help at all? So, during the course of the visit, Martha was challenged with single-handedly serving the crowd. Now, anyone who has hosted a dinner party, for even as few as six people, knows this was not a small feat. Nevertheless, Martha, albeit anxious and distracted, was doing her best.

Many of us are familiar with what I imagine to be a soft-spoken scolding, such as Martha received from Jesus (Luke 10:41–42). This reproof, concerning her little outburst, was Jesus's way of instructing Martha about how to have a *great* day. I believe Martha was already having a nice day. Anytime you can spend your day in the service of our Lord it's a good day. The one distinction that would make it a great day is being *aware* while in the presence of the Lord. In Luke 10:40 several translations define Martha as being distracted. The distinction begs two questions. Distracted from what? And distracted by what?

Clearly Martha drew away from listening to Jesus teach. Surely Martha's desire was to be taught by the Master, but having a strong propensity to serve, she initially made the wrong choice of action. These two sisters were faced with the same decision, but one chose to sit and enjoy Jesus's presence, and the other chose to serve Jesus and His disciples.

Jesus without a doubt, prefers our
intimacy with Him over our service to Him.

In Luke 10:42 NIV, Jesus distinctly states which of the sisters made the "better" choice. Mary took the smarter option when she positioned herself at Jesus's feet, not missing a word. Martha, on the other hand, missed much that day. She missed the opportunity to have an intimate encounter with Jesus. Jesus was open with Martha, and anyone else who might have been listening.

At one time I would have argued on Martha's behalf. If it were not for Martha, no one would have eaten that day. Eventually, I realized that Jesus was accustomed to spontaneously feeding much larger crowds than this assembly.

Jesus was not saying that serving is wrong, but He was quick to lovingly point out, when service precedes intimacy with Him, it will be filled with anxiety and worry. Intimacy with Jesus prepares us to serve Him and others graciously. When we've taken the time to sit at the feet of Jesus, thus having a Mary Morning, our service becomes free of worry and offense. This unique time in the presence of the Lord helps us prioritize our acts of service and good deeds for the day. We start with His hand of blessing on what we will be doing throughout our day. He relieves us of the tasks that are not beneficial within the precious time He gives us.

Martha, as you might imagine, was a quick study. She learns much from this day of being overwhelmed to the point of inciting Jesus to scold her sister. Other passages in the Bible recount Martha's continued unruffled service to the Lord during the week before His crucifixion.

I would also venture to say that Mary, Martha, and Lazarus put Bethany on the map for all of history. Jesus repeatedly treks to Bethany to visit His friends and relax after spending time at the temple in Jerusalem. Jesus's actions create a groundswell of believers who eventually come to recognize Him as the Messiah. Martha plainly explains, in John 11:27, "'Yes, Lord,' she told him, 'I believe you are the Messiah, the Son of God, who comes into the world.'" John 11:24 says, "Martha said to him, 'I know that he will rise again in the resurrection at the last day.'" Martha's exchange with Jesus, about her brother Lazarus's death, in John 11:21, reveals what she knows and what she believes as she proclaims the gospel: "If you had been here, my brother wouldn't have died." Martha didn't come by this revelation of truth by preparing meals and picking up dirty dishes. At some point Martha would have had to spend time at Jesus's feet for this knowledge to have been imparted to her. In Luke 10:22, Jesus said, "All things have been entrusted to me by my Father. No one knows who the Son is except the Father, and who the Father is except the Son, and anyone to whom the Son desires to reveal him." Martha had her very own "Mary moment."

In Bethany, at the home of Simon the leper, Mary anoints Jesus with costly oil. It was six days before the Passover. We find all the siblings sharing in this gathering among friends. Mary is anointing. Lazarus is reclining. Martha is serving. Martha seems so predictable, unable to stop herself from doing what servants do. I wonder if it even occurred to Martha that the supper at Simon's house was an opportunity to have the night off and behave as a guest. I feel like I know Martha. She is likely most comfortable when serving. She's not about to miss out on serving "the Messiah, the Son of God." Of course, Martha saw this evening as a chance to honor both her Lord and her friends.

Mary, as predictable as her sister, is doing what Mary does best and, inevitably, causes us all to want to be more like her. She is demonstrating her love for Jesus by pouring an entire bottle of expensive perfume on His head and feet. Mary then wipes up the excess with her hair. John 12 tells us she used a pound of perfume, which gives us some idea of Mary's lavish extravagance. What an expression of love for our Lord. Jesus made a declaration in response to Mary's extravagant gesture in the Gospel of Matthew,

"Wherever the gospel is proclaimed in the whole world, what she has done will also be told in memory of her."

All four Gospel accounts attest to Jesus's two-mile triumphal entry into Jerusalem, just days before His crucifixion. At the evening's conclusion Jesus retreats once again into the comfort and familiarity of His friends in the little village of Bethany. He repeats this routine of retreating to Bethany two more days and nights, then spends the night before His arrest in the garden of Gethsemane. These events occurred just after the last supper with His disciples.

After His arrest, things begin to happen quickly—the trial, His crucifixion, burial, and resurrection. The final time Jesus is physically seen in the Scriptures and on earth is in Martha and Mary's hometown. Jesus leads the disciples and the others who gathered with them out to Bethany for His ascension in Luke 24:50–51, "Then he led them out to the vicinity of Bethany, and lifting up his hands he blessed them. And while he was blessing them, he left them and was carried up into heaven. After worshiping him, they returned to Jerusalem with great joy." These accounts highlight how important these two women were to Jesus.

∞ ∞ ∞

MARTHA-MARY REFLECTIONS

Take a moment to explore the Scripture mentioned in this chapter, familiarizing yourself with how often Jesus chose to visit Martha, Mary, and Lazarus.

After doing so, focus on the following questions.

1. What do you think makes Mary, Martha, and Lazarus friends of Jesus?

2. Why do you think Jesus keeps coming back to their home in Bethany?

3. Do you naturally behave more like Martha or Mary, and why do you think that is true?

4. What do you admire about Martha in the Gospel account in Luke 10?

5. What do you admire about Mary in the Gospel account in Luke 10?

2

THE ΛCT OF SEEKING

∞ ∞ ∞

S pending time alone with God can be easier said than done. I have struggled with trying to make it a sustainable and enjoyable part of my life. Intimacy with God eluded me for many years, but in recognizing and valuing the endless benefits from encounters with a living, loving God, I pressed on. Also, knowing the enemy did not want me to enjoy anything concerning our God spurred me on to pursue what Jesus calls His "best" treasure. Best, of course, was the aspect of sitting at the feet of Jesus, the act that came so naturally to Mary.

For years I tried setting aside time first thing in the morning. I succeeded but only for a while. Eventually, like so many times before, the act of sitting alone with God would become an unpleasant chore that required my attention much too early. Next I put my "God chore" at the end of my day. Before long it was the laborious task that stood between my tired body and my pillow. I've also tried after breakfast, during my lunch break, and I've even tried talking to God on my drives into work. Each attempt ended in defeat, and I would start the entire cycle over again. I repeated this inane behavior for several years before I could claim even a marginal victory in either of the areas of discipline or devotion.

I wanted so badly to have special times with my Lord Jesus. Some days I would start with prayer only to get distracted and end up making a mental to-do list. Other times I would begin by reading Scripture only to end up mindlessly reading large passages without a clear understanding of what I read. In many instances I felt like I was just going through the motions. But one day I realized I was at least being more consistent. Eventually I invested in written spiritual materials that gave me various options to keep my time with God interesting.

The discovery of devotionals and topic-specific books created an excitement about meeting with God first thing in the morning. I used independent Bible studies on subjects like prayer, worship, or a particular book of the Bible. I created special spaces, both outside and inside my home, and later added soft instrumental music to the experience. With each addition I found I enjoyed this special time more and more. I started waking up earlier and earlier in eager expectation. I began hearing from God on specific matters and feeling an intense spiritual connection with Him. I consistently jotted notes in a journal, recording what the Holy Spirit was teaching me. One of my favorite devotional books is *My Utmost for His Highest* by Oswald Chambers. It challenged my spiritual growth considerably.

Morning after morning, instead of only verbalizing, I wrote my prayers to God. I was now thoroughly comfortable sitting still in the presence of the Holy Spirit while the Lord ministered to me. I know this led me to hear from God more often.

Nowadays my time with God, on any given day, may consist of:

Prayer

Worship

Reading Scripture

Studying the Word

Singing

Journaling

Meditating on the Word

Sitting still in His presence

Hearing from the Lord

Imagine enjoying true intimacy with the God of the universe, the One who overcame the world. Picture yourself receiving His instructions, direction, clarity, and wisdom. Where else could you possibly want to be in the early morning than in His presence?

Jesus wants to complete the great work He started in us, but it takes our cooperation. We must make ourselves available to Him by learning His Word and His way. We must become students under the divine tutelage of the Holy Spirit. After all, we spend ample time in the world, learning its ways and systems. How much time are we making ourselves available so the Holy Spirit can train us in the way we should go as His sons and daughters?

I'm sure, if we are honest enough with ourselves, we can admit we all have certain areas within ourselves that could benefit from change. The Bible refers to this process as being "transformed by the renewing of your mind" (Rom. 12:2).These changes don't happen by wishing it so. They require a new way of thinking.

Renewing the mind erases old faulty
thinking and replaces those ideas with the
truth of God's Word.

To know this truth—His truth—you must spend time with the life-giving, life-changing Word. "Do not be conformed to this age, but be transformed by the renewing of your mind, so that you may discern what is the good, pleasing, and perfect will of God" (Rom. 12:2).

∞ ∞ ∞

Heaven is our home. We are not citizens of this world. We need to set our sights on the spiritual world because we are essentially spiritual beings. The easiest way, I've found, to achieve this end is to have Mary mornings. Deciding to make Jesus the center of your attention and keeping Him in the forefront of your mind throughout the day are two different things to master. If you don't do the first, it is tough to accomplish the second. Some mornings I find myself humming an old hymn that goes like this, "I woke up this mornin' with my mind stayed on Jesus, Hallelu! Hallelu! Hallelujah!" I like rejoicing in the Lord when I wake up. My first thoughts are of Jesus and His goodness. If you can stay your mind on Jesus and keep it trained on Him, you'll see your circumstances in the light of His truths. The Jesus mind-set will dispel fear and anxiety.

My quiet times with God are cherished moments. Those moments are the only protected part of the day when I don't have anywhere else to be. I have no other agenda except to be with God. I have granted myself permission not to think about the rest of my day or try to solve any of its problems unless the Holy Spirit brings up something. If the Holy Spirit introduces a problem I've been concerned about, He is usually presenting me with a solution or sense of peace. I can always rest assured He is working things out for my good. "Let me experience your faithful love in the morning, for I trust in you. Reveal to me the way I should go because I appeal to you" (Ps. 143:8).

Oh, how God wants to connect with us in a meaningful way!

Time spent with the Lord is a tender time of receiving from Him that which you need emotionally, spiritually, and physically.

Your life will be enriched because of intimacy with Him.

God wants to impart so many truths to us, as well as blessings He wants us to reach out and accept. We cannot fathom the vastness of everything He has to offer inside His love. The Lord wants to expand our thinking, beliefs, and faith so that we can comprehend the full meaning and measure of His compassion and His grace.

My response is to get down on my knees before the Father, this magnificent Father who parcels out all heaven and earth. I ask him to strengthen you by his Spirit—not a brute strength but a glorious inner strength—that Christ will live in you as you open the door and invite him in. And I ask him that with both feet planted firmly on love, you'll be able to take in with all followers of Jesus the extravagant dimensions of

Christ's love. Reach out and experience the breadth!
Test its length! Plumb the depths! Rise to the heights!
Live full lives, full in the fullness of God. (Eph. 3:14–19
MSG)

We must realize our God (the Father of time) does not clamor for minutes or hours, as we mere mortals do. How foolish must we sound to Him when we say we don't have time for this or that? Every second we have as human beings is given to us by God. He even gives us the most effective time management principle in Matthew 6:33 (KJV), "But seek first the kingdom of God and his righteousness, and all these things will be provided for you." "These things" can take our attention away from Him. "These things" can cause us to worry and become anxious. Jesus never disapproved of Martha's service. He merely wanted her service to be in proper order and without worry and anxiety. Her desire to serve our Lord was admirable, but it had become tainted and worthy of reprimand at the point she started complaining. Let's agree not to let our complaining and bad attitude undo our good deeds.

MARTHA-MARY REFLECTIONS

Read and meditate on Romans 12:2. After doing so, focus on the following questions.

1. What has first place in your life today?

2. What would seeking God's kingdom *first* look like in your life?

3. What distracts you from having a quiet time?

4. Are you willing to commit to the time it will take to renew your mind in specific areas as God leads you?

5. If you have a Mary personality, or have become more like Mary regarding spending alone time with God, what are some things you've done to cultivate your quiet time.

3

CHIEF MARTHA AMONG US

∞ ∞ ∞

Embracing the reality that I am naturally more Martha minded than Mary minded is my first step to balance in my life. I came into this world a Martha, or it could be the fact that I am second in a sibling chain of eight. Older siblings of large families are generally given more responsibility earlier in life than their younger sisters and brothers. Let's face it—typically Marthas are planners, problem solvers, and project-oriented people. We wake up with our to-do list prominently on our mind, juggling ideas as to the order best suited to accomplish the tasks. We are not likely to ask for help unless we are feeling completely overwhelmed. Those pleas for help may sound more like demands, criticism, or complaints. Unfortunately most of us are so self-consumed with activities that we live our lives absent of the awe-inspiring awareness that we are, in fact, still journeying with

Jesus. We are not alone. He has not left us to fend for ourselves, even if our actions reflect otherwise.

Consequently, we continue to make plans from our puny perspective, which is one dimensional and perhaps two dimensional if we have family interests to consider. The results of failing to include Jesus are often the same for every Martha. We miss out (*big time)* on the best plan for our lives. We go out and live mediocre lives when we could be living truly, incredible lives, the life Jesus planned and died for us to have. "I have come so that they may have life and have it in abundance" (John 10:10).

Allow me to submit, there is a much better way to start each day. Why not try the Mary way? Let me encourage you to slow your pace before you go dashing out the door, unprepared for the day's challenges. You may be thinking, *How can I slow my pace when everything on my proverbial plate is urgent and time's a wasting?* But take it from me, the chief Martha among all Marthas. There is a much better way, guaranteed to maximize your plans and alleviate most of your problems, even before they become concerns.

The Mary way will make you one of the most
highly productive people on the planet.

Sounds like music to your little Martha ears? Before you get too geeked, let me caution you, it will take a bit of effort. If it were easy, all followers of Jesus Christ would be victorious in this area and thrive in spiritual maturity. Consider Jesus's disciples when He instructed them to pray, only to return and find them asleep (Luke 22). But once you have mastered the Mary way, you will likely not go back to your old way of doing things. I am convinced, if you let Jesus in on the planning stage early in the morning, He will make your path level and make short order of your lists and tasks. "I will go before you and level the uneven places" (Isa. 45:2).

Your challenge is to take one step further. Why not go beyond giving God the first part of your day and trusting Him with your entire day to orchestrate as He desires? Nothing on this earth will offer you absolute freedom and peace of mind like giving your day (the same one He just gave you) to almighty God. This single gesture creates an instant openness of mind and expectation. Your load will be decidedly lighter because you are handing it over to God. Your focus shifts away from your problems; instead you are intently watching how God will develop your day and the roles He wants you to play. Now, in all honesty, you may need many tries and many failures to get this right. Our flesh (or carnal nature) still wants to lead. I know I've hit that spot when I hear myself saying things like:

"Why am I doing all the work?"

"I don't have time for this!"

"Where is everyone else?"

You'll realize pretty quickly: I'm not only spoiling my mood but also grieving the Holy Spirit in the process.

As a planner who wants to be pleasing to Christ Jesus, I must constantly evaluate my intentions. Occasionally a lack of trust or even fear causes me to begin to sure things up with my own self-made, solid plan. In the mind of a Martha, good planning requires analyzing a situation from various angles and even making room for the unexpected and always having a plan B or backup plan. Compulsive planning can be problematic if it is not tempered with trust and the ability to leave the outcome to the Lord.

There is nothing wrong with being a Martha. Jesus proved that by His repeated visits to Bethany. We have to admire Martha for being so flexible with her routine that she was able to invite Jesus and company into her home spontaneously. When you find your routine wants to dictate your day's activity, challenge it by asking yourself the following questions: "Am I doing this out of habit? Am I where I'm supposed to be, doing what God has instructed me to do?"

Don't be afraid of getting out of your routine, no matter how efficient it seems to be. God's will and His ways are perfect. They will not fail you. Marthas, on the other hand, can and do fail to acknowledge His will, fail to execute His will, and even sometimes fail to yield to His will. We desperately believe we need to do things our way. We must recognize our "smarts" come from His infinite intelligence. Our common sense comes from His eternal wealth of wisdom. And yes, our know-how comes from and is an itty-bitty fraction of His all-knowing consciousness. "God—his way is perfect; the word of the LORD is pure. He is a shield to all who take refuge in Him" (Ps. 18:30).

∞ ∞ ∞

"God—he clothes me with strength and makes my way perfect" (Ps. 18:32). Examining why I'm doing a certain thing and how it makes me feel empowers me to quickly eliminate unnecessary busyness from my day. When reviewing these things in the sight of God, I am amazed at how clear they become. I can see what needs to fill my day and what does not. The Martha in me always puts more into my day than is reasonably possible. But with God as my daily witness, I am able to whittle down my lists to the bare necessities.

We will inevitably have to allow Him to prune away all the unnecessary tasks we've piled on ourselves—many times for appearance's sake. There, I've said it. If we're truthful, many of the things we do are for appearances alone. If we were to look at our to-do list intently, most of us would have to admit Jesus is not the only One we are trying to impress. Check your motive continually. Don't be tempted to add to a task unless you can honestly say it is in service to Christ. I am always grateful to have the Holy Spirit for additional insight into situations.

God is not impressed with our busyness. It probably saddens Him, much as it does a child when a parent doesn't have time for him or her. How did we get so busy? At what point did it become cool to be too busy to accomplish all that we take on? I once heard it put this way, "We tend to wear busyness like a badge of honor." It squeezes God out of our lives. It puts us in a position that inhibits us from hearing and receiving from God.

Hearing from God requires a still mind,
a listening ear, and a receiving heart.

The Martha in me keeps me from admitting that my circumstances are overwhelming me. It can cause me to deny my weaknesses. But in my Mary mornings I seem to have no trouble admitting to God how frail and inadequate I feel. Realizing Jesus knows my limitations and what I'm made of is liberating. In these moments I am quick to admit my desire to work His plan and not my own. Rejoice in His superiority and perfection. Every Martha I know wants the best, most efficient plan. The result of planning in the presence of God is peace.

When you are alone with God, transparency must rule the conversation. You are conversing with the One who reads your heart and knows your thoughts. In turn you're going to have to get real with yourself. This self-transparency allows you to examine your emotions and motives honestly.

> LORD, you have searched me and known me.
>
> You know when I sit down and when I stand up;
>
> you understand my thoughts from far away.
>
> You observe my travels and my rest;
>
> you are aware of all my ways.
>
> Before a word is on my tongue,
>
> you know all about it, LORD.
>
> You have encircled me;
>
> you have placed your hand on me.
>
> This wondrous knowledge is beyond me.
>
> It is lofty; I am unable to reach it. (Ps. 139:1–6)

∞ ∞ ∞

Allow me to give you a word of caution; avoid reaching for tomorrow's worries in the planning stage, it can be disruptive and problematic. Otherwise, the process of planning can be freeing and fun—freeing in the sense that we can get everything off our minds, by moving it onto paper and calendar. We no longer have to burden ourselves with remembering all the details. Also, the wonderful ideas, supplied by the Holy Spirit, bless us.

"God is my helper; the Lord is the sustainer of my life" (Ps. 54:4). We should draw heavily on the Holy Spirit when making lists, seeking His counsel in the process, whether a guest list, grocery list, or a standard to-do list. I am mindful always to ask two questions: "What else, Lord? Who else, Lord?" Pausing to hear from the Holy Spirit on various matters takes the anxiety out of the process, lest I forget something or, worse, someone. Collaborating with my Lord about how to prepare for the day is fun whether I'm planning an event, a gathering, or a vacation. Including the Lord ensures arrangements will be special for everyone involved. Did you notice? I didn't say *perfect* for everyone but *special* for everyone. When I stopped making perfection the goal and turned my attention to everyone's enjoyment, I became an artist at hosting memorable events, similar to those I suppose Martha was accustomed to hosting.

If anything will sabotage and plummet a high-spirited mood, it's the anxiety and fretting of the host or hostess. Just as Jesus checked Martha, I rely on the Holy Spirit to keep me in check. He is quick to let me know when I am fussing over something or have become obsessive about the wrong things. After all, the participants are mostly taking their cues from the organizer or host. Staying on an even keel and remaining gracious sets the tone, helps participants feel included, and makes the entire event more comfortable for everyone.

If the proper planning is done with the Holy Spirit's involvement, leaving the outcome to God is easy. Even if something is overlooked, a quick evaluation of its importance usually concludes the lack thereof, knowing the Holy Spirit would have brought it to my mind earlier if it really mattered. The Holy Spirit and I are in it together.

Lastly, getting God's permission to take on additional assignments is paramount. I aim to consult Him during the entire planning process, from permission to fruition. Together the Holy Spirit and I can cohost all life events graciously, ensuring the proper outcome. Joy!

MARTHA-MARY REFLECTIONS

Read Psalm 139. Then proceed to these questions.

1. Are you willing to hand over the reins and start letting God steer your life, and if yes, what is the first step you will make in that direction?

2. In what way(s) are you ready to be flexible and give God permission to interrupt your routine?

3. Are you ready to admit your frailties and inadequacies to God? If yes, take the time to do that now.

4. At this season in your life, what is your role in God's master plan, and are you willing to play your part?

5. Are you prepared to examine your motives in every situation, and how will that change the way you approach your decision making?

4

GOOD, BETTER, OR BEST?

∞ ∞ ∞

Good old common sense could probably help most people make relatively good decisions, but when I request the help of the Holy Spirit, I make consistently better decisions. Consider the progression of good, better, and best. Who settles for good when best is so attainable? If we shun genuine relationship and intimacy with God because we are too busy or too preoccupied, what does that say about our decision-making ability?

God has a plan for each and every one of us. His plan for our lives is perfect. His agenda is far superior to our own. While you entertain what you consider to be *your* dreams, they are often the result of the desires God has placed within you. Even your ultimate plan is only a minuscule glimpse of what God has envisioned for you. Why would anyone want anything other than God's way? Allow me to give you my insight.

Generally, God doesn't choose to show us the whole start-to-finish plan surrounding our dreams. Sadly, many of us will not follow Him unless we know precisely where we are going. It's a trust issue, plain and simple. Jesus instructs us to follow Him. But we tend to want specifics. Hence, where to? He has our destiny and our specific destinations in His hands. For this to work, we must first trust and believe with all our hearts that God's plan is better than our own simple plans. We must believe He genuinely loves us unconditionally and has our best interests at heart. After all, He promises to give us the desires of our hearts.

According to Isaiah 55:9, God, says, "My ways are higher than your ways and my thoughts than your thoughts." Psalm 37:4 tells us to "take delight in the LORD, and he will give you your heart's desires." I believe this not only means God will give us the things we desire but also that the desire that is stirring in our hearts is put there by God. And who wants to see us achieve our heart's desire more than God Himself? Where did your love for music, cooking, or math originate? You may say, "I've always had it, ever since I was a kid" My point, exactly. The desire seems to have always been there as if you were born with it. It's probably not something you have ever nurtured very much; it's been there as long as you can remember.

∞ ∞ ∞

Your passions are God-given desires.

Do you think God would give you desires or dreams He didn't intend on helping you to obtain or achieve? Would parents pay a registration fee for their child to participate in a sport if they didn't intend to get the child to the practices, games, and purchase their uniform? No one wants a child to enjoy and succeed at sports more than the parents. Likewise, who wants you to accomplish what you were created to do even more than you? God, your Creator.

Martha types tend to be activators. They need to be busy and planning for the expected as well as the unexpected. That's where worry usually invades the scene. Thinking and rethinking a thing becomes our own undoing. Our actions can be a huge display of lack of trust in our Creator God, Sustainer of all things, including the details of our little lives. What an insult to our Lord who came to earth, lived a perfect life, willingly died on the cross for our sins, and rose from the dead so that we could experience abundant life, free from worry and fear. And He is *still* in charge. He didn't relinquish His lordship or put someone else in charge. He certainly didn't put you or me in charge. We are His servants; He is our Lord.

At this point not being in charge is a relief. I'm thrilled that I'm not responsible for the success of it all, whatever "all" happens to be. What a relief! Following the instructions of the Holy Spirit helps me stay on the path that God has prepared specifically for me. This way I can walk out His perfect plan and experience an abundant life, filled with His joy and peace.

My Father knows what I need each and every day. Today is no exception. He made me. He made the day. He made everything I will need to carry out His plan for me today. So, why worry? Why fret? Why should I concern myself over the when and how? Why not wait on the Lord to reveal all these things in His exact time? "For it was you who created my inward parts; you knit me together in my mother's womb. I will praise you because I have been remarkably and wondrously made. Your works are wondrous and I know this very well" (Ps. 139:13–14).

The God who knitted us together in our mother's womb not only wants us to know and do His will; He also wants us to know Him—really know Him. Not just know *of* Him or *about* Him but know Him intimately. Mary mornings are all about our Creator God and seeking Him for His plan. Psalm 37:23 shows us, "A person's steps are established by the LORD, and he takes pleasure in his way." So, if the Lord has already established my steps, wouldn't it behoove me to seek Him for guidance and direction? I believe that the best time to ask for directions is before you start. Why wait until you are utterly lost? Likewise, why wait until your day is coming apart at the seams before you turn to God and ask Him to show you the way? It's not that our way has not been established. It is our failure to ask Him to lead us where and instruct us how to proceed.

We must have the presence of mind to ask
for His guidance and then to follow His lead.

When you live in a large city, as I do, one would hardly leave home without checking the traffic report or Waze to get around traffic. Why would anyone who has access to the most powerful Being in the universe ignore seeking Him for direction? He is the same One who has gone before you and is also your active rear guard. He takes great pleasure in illuminating your path. Why do we neglect to stop and download our directions for the day from God Himself? He is never too busy for us. He is not playing hide-and-seek with us. Quite the contrary, He says to seek Him, and He shall be found. "I love them that love me; and those that seek me early shall find me" (Prov. 8:17 KJV).

God's Word serves as the lamp that shines a light on our path. Why stumble around in the dark, as if no light was ever provided? We must open "the Good Book," God's Holy Scripture, and learn from Him. "Your word is a lamp for my feet and a light on my path" (Ps. 119:105).

If we sought after the Lord in the same way we pursued perfection, a career, or a mate, not only would we achieve all of these in the process, but also the pursuit of them would be more fulfilling. The Holy Spirit is the best company keeper. He is full of good advice. He is patient and sees much farther up the road than we can. He is insightful and warns us. His infinite wisdom is there for the asking. Why would one go through life ignoring such a special Friend? "But seek first the kingdom of God and his righteousness, and all these things shall be provided for you" (Matt. 6:33).

∞ ∞ ∞

In Psalms 32:7–8, King David says, "You are my hiding place; you protect me from trouble. You surround me with joyful shouts of deliverance." In this exchange between David and His Lord, God responds, "I will instruct you and show you the way to go; with my eye on you, I will give counsel" (v. 8). Does this sound like God is hard to find? Jesus also said, in Matthew 7:7, "Ask and it will be given to you. Seek, and you will find. Knock, and the door will be opened to you." In our materialistic world, many of us assume the Scripture refers to asking for *things*, and it does to some extent. But how much more powerful is this privilege when we consider asking for wisdom, godly knowledge, insight, discernment, and other spiritual gifts? One successful day after another, strung together, equates to a successful life journey. Conversely, when you lose sight of God day after day, succumbing to your circumstances is easy. Stay connected to Him. You can remain above your circumstances with a fresh perspective from God.

Imagine a toddler snatching his hand away from his parent in a crowded sports arena. The toddler can see only the kneecaps of the adults surrounding him. He can't see the exit signs, restrooms, or refreshments. The toddler can't even discern who are the ushers or attendants in the arena. He is totally dependent on his parent to lead him through the maze of people towering overhead. We all know how the scene ends. The child eventually cries out, looking frantically for his parent and the guidance he originally rejected.

Why do we wait until we are totally exhausted and lost before we decide to seek His guidance? Martha didn't need Mary's help. She needed Jesus's help to lighten her load or, better yet, to help her discern how much to take on in the first place. How often do we hear the words, "Let me help you" or "You can depend on me"? It's rare and getting rarer. Jesus, on the other hand, practically begs us not to go it alone but to follow Him, to lean on Him, to bring our burdens to Him, and to cast our cares on Him. We have two choices: we can stress and agonize over making and implementing our own plans, or we can choose to yield to God's perfect plan for our lives.

The Martha in me embraces the light burden and easy yoke my Lord's plan has to offer. In Matthew 11:28–30, Jesus invites us to "come to me, all of you who are weary and burdened, and I will give you rest. Take up my yoke and learn of me, because I am lowly and humble in heart, and you will find rest for your souls. For my yoke is easy and my burden is light." Sign me up. If there is one thing this Martha is always seeking, it is an easier way to accomplish what needs to be done. In case you missed your new to-do list, here is the abbreviated version:

- Don't go it alone.
- Bring your burdens to Jesus.
- Yield to God's plan for your life. It's perfect.
- Take the rest Jesus is offering

MARTHA-MARY REFLECTIONS

Read and meditate on Isaiah 55:9 and Psalm 37:4. Now reflect on the questions below.

1. What consumes your day and causes you to miss out on God's best for you?

2. What is your God-given desire or passion? Is there more than one?

3. What are some ways God shows you He loves you individually?

4. Describe a time when you felt like God had just kept you from danger?

5. Can you think of a time when your plan didn't work out, but when you looked back on the situation, you could see that God had a plan that worked out far better?

5

ACCESSING OUR POWER

∞ ∞ ∞

Imagine starting your days feeling immeasurably loved and immensely empowered to accomplish anything. A sense of victory comes, not because of your abilities but because you have access to an unlimited supply of God's love and power. Romans 8:31 says: "If God is for us, who is against us?" Confidence and awareness of this truth fosters strength in our being. Your persona would be altogether different if you embraced what the Word of God says about you.

I believe people are attracted to the glorious light that exudes from God's people. The world may recognize this as confidence. Just sitting in the presence of God causes the mind to be renewed by degrees, shifting our problems into proper perspective. He is infinitely bigger than any problem we may perceive. "When I am filled with cares, your comfort brings me joy" (Ps. 94:19).

When I am keenly aware God is with me, calmness rushes over me. The particulars don't matter in any given situation I find myself entertaining. Whether I am struggling through mundane tasks or I am at the height of contention, the awareness of His never-changing truth trumps all my emotions. As a type of Martha, I tend to be high-energy personality. But knowing God is with me has a way of stabilizing me and stepping me into a comfortable cadence. In the presence of God, I feel the lavishness of His love for me. Lingering longer with the Lord is a sure way to make any ordinary day an extraordinary day. When the pure love of God is interjected into a situation, it corrects any perceived problem that crops up throughout the day. You come away knowing how to handle life lovingly.

Another trait of the "Martha syndrome" can be the constant need to be doing something. This tendency is diabolically opposed to "quiet time" or "resting in the presence of God." Marthas are accustomed to serving and ministering to others. They need to focus on setting aside time with God to be ministered to and replenished by God Himself. "He renews my life: he leads me alone the right paths for his name's sake" (Ps. 23:3).

Sometimes stilling the soul and quieting the spirit can be the most difficult part of spending time with God. Our minds race with thoughts. Our flesh wants to be doing something else, anything else. Our souls and spirits can feel hijacked and forced to go along with what appears to be an unprofitable investment of time. I had to resolve to let the world go on without me because I knew the best medicine was to allow my Lord to restore my soul. Only then can I feel my limbs relax and my mind shifting into low gear and then down into neutral. I receive the much-needed nourishment my soul and spirit crave. When you feel empty or anxious, do this first, before you try anything else. Slow down and get a healthy dose of the presence of God, receiving "love, joy, peace, patience, kindness, goodness, faithfulness, gentleness, and self-control" (Gal. 5:22–23).

Breathe it all in.

Once you are restored and filled, you will be equipped to go out into the world and benefit others.

You are no longer the needy one, but you are now the one who meets the needs of others. You are no longer frantic but the one who exhibits peace and gives encouragement. You are able to pour from the abundance of God's love and joy in your life into the lives of others.

The world is full of hurting people. They don't need more of the same; they need to know the Jesus that lives in us. Will you introduce them to Him? "There is nowhere God is not. We are always in His Presence because He is everywhere. But, there is also something very distinct about being still that makes us intensely aware of the robe of righteousness that drapes over us. His everlasting love permeates our very essence. I rejoice greatly in the LORD, I exult in my God; for he hath clothed me with the garments of salvation and wrapped me in a robe of righteousness" (Isa. 61:10).

I've found living in this awareness increases my self-awareness and intentionality. When I say "self-aware," I don't mean *self-absorbed.* I'm talking about self-awareness, in the sense of purpose and how God uses a yielded vessel. Living while mindful of God's desire to use us, along with His intentions for us to make an impact for His kingdom, causes us to scrutinize the use of our time and resources. The anticipation of being used by God, at any moment of any given day, heightens our level of attentiveness and, therefore, our zeal for life.

A commitment on our part to live yielded to
the Holy Spirit's guidance is a sure way to
enhance this experience we call life.

Practicing the act of remaining in the presence of God takes perseverance. Keeping our minds continually cognizant of the Holy Spirit is no small feat. It takes time to develop. Be patient with yourself. After all He is your Helper. Ask for His help with this spiritual discipline. As you train your thoughts toward this state of awareness, it will become more natural. It is next to impossible to worry and be aware of the Lord's presence simultaneously. These two frames of mind cannot coexist. So, which would you rather do? Wallow in your worries or stand in His presence and power?

The presence of Jesus pulverizes my problems. Awareness of His presence annihilates anxiety. Reminding myself that "He is with me" sends worry right out the window. When the light of His presence illuminates my mind, problems, anxiety, and worry melt away—not because the problem that causes anxiety or worry is gone but because I know I am not alone to handle it by myself. The great I Am lives inside of us, and His wisdom and infinite knowledge of all things past, present, and future are made available to us if we will just seek Him for ways to resolve problems.

Now I'm in a seeker mode instead of a worry mode. What a difference this shift makes on a person's perspective. It's the difference in being Mary minded, seeking Jesus, or being Martha minded, worrying about problems Jesus already has the answer to if I would just focus my attention on Him. Resolve to stay in seeker mode. Following Jesus and allowing Him to lead us to a solution makes for a Martha kind of day.

∞ ∞ ∞

Mary mornings are my way of intentionally connecting with the Holy Spirit. Making this bond early in the morning allows me to benefit from it all day long. Taking shortcuts and avoiding pitfalls makes for a highly productive, full-of-momentum Martha kind of day. Now that doesn't just happen because I've given my Lord the first part of my day; I must remain attentive to the leading of His Spirit throughout the day.

My new vocation becomes listening for His whispers of instructions, watching for His hand in matters, and sensing His movement to ensure I don't miss an opportunity, and of course praying constantly (1 Thess. 5:16). This posture of prayer and being in constant communication with the Holy Spirit keeps me attentive and yielding to His will and not my own. "Pray constantly, give thanks in everything; for this is God's will for you in Christ Jesus" (1 Thess. 5:17–18).

∞ ∞ ∞

When I turn my spiritual ear to hear Jesus early in the morning, I'm more inclined to hear Him throughout the day. When I rush out and begin my day in a hurry, I do more talking to myself and others and find myself looking for things. I seem to be in a more agitated state of mind, and everything needs my attention now. I hear myself saying things like: "Where is my . . . ?" "Where did I put my . . . ?" or "Oh, I forgot!" And in all my rushing around, I'm still late to the meeting and have forgotten what I was supposed to bring.

Jesus wants us to depend on Him entirely,
not only when we think we can't handle life.

Dependency has almost become a derogatory term in our society. Independence, on the other hand, is a common goal. We strive to develop our children's independence as quickly as possible. But when it comes to Christ, independence is challenged, and even shunned, as a rebellious spirit. How can we reconcile the contrast? Jesus doesn't want us seeking, leaning, and depending on other people. He wants us to reserve our neediness for Him and Him alone. Jesus wants to supply our needs. He urges us to exchange our independence for a life of dependency on Him and the Holy Spirit. "And my God will supply all your needs according to his riches in glory in Christ Jesus" (Phil. 4:19).

This way of thinking can be specifically troublesome for the Marthas of the world. My dear sister, Martha, I know all too well the adage, "If you want something done right, you might as well do it yourself." It has served us well. But, if we are honest with ourselves, it also wears us out. How can we talk about the Martha mind-set without addressing the need to control? Control is not completely bad, particularly regarding our thoughts, tongue, or bad habits. Where these are concerned, exercising self-control is admirable, but overall control is a facade. We may have a plan that gives us a certain sense of control, but at the first sign of trouble, we are forced to concede to the fact that our plan is imperfect.

Trouble has a way of exposing the fact that we are just as needy as the next person. Recognizing the necessity of our dependency on Jesus is one of the sanest observations we can make. Depending on Jesus is not only the smart thing to do, but it's also easier than trying to do everything yourself, inside your own frail strength. I encourage you not to wait until your strength diminishes before you tap into God's strength. His strength is inexhaustible, giving you the power to do all things in Him. "I am able to do all things through him who strengthens me" (Phil. 4:13).

MARTHA-MARY REFLECTIONS

Read and meditate on Isaiah 61:10a. Now reflect on the questions below.

1. What is keeping you from making Jesus the center of your attention?

2. How long are you willing to linger in the loving presence of God before you let your problems take a bow to the Lord?

3. What are some ways the Holy Spirit is teaching you to relieve your frustrations?

4. How will you develop the presence of mind to interrupt your day and consult the Lord for His great guidance when things take an unexpected turn?

5. How will you perform heart checks off and on during the day to make sure you are not out of step with God?

6

BEING MARY

∞ ∞ ∞

The best part about spending Mary mornings basking in the presence of my Lord Jesus is the resounding feeling of love that permeates my spirit being. As His pure and perfect love washes over me, it washes away my fear, doubt, and anxiety. I'm able to rest in the tranquility of the moment. All my ruffled feathers settle back down. My mind and spirit begin to engage in a two-step type dance—love and gratitude, gratitude and love, both overwhelming me and sweeping me off my feet. I know I've experienced a Mary morning because my brand of Martha is much too serious to dance.

Delighting in the Lord is one thing, but knowing and understanding that the Lord also delights in you is another! You may have difficulty imagining this, but just as He loved us before we loved Him, Jesus took great delight in us before we knew what it was to delight in the Lord. "Let them praise his name in the dancing and make music to him with the tambourine and lyre. For the LORD takes pleasure in his people; he adorns the humble with salvation" (Ps. 149:3–4).

The idea thrills me that Jesus gets as much enjoyment and delight out of our set-aside time together as I do. If you can get your mind around this truth early in the morning, it will reshape your day.

God can be anywhere and is everywhere in the universe, yet He relishes one-on-one time with me.

Mary positioned herself at the feet of Jesus to receive His teaching firsthand. We, too, can receive daily instruction, direction, wise counsel, and empowerment from Jesus. If we forgo this time of receiving from God, we not only go out misguided, but we miss the pleasures and fullness of joy we can receive in His presence.

How can we walk out the door knowing we've left our most important life tool behind? Our addiction to busyness can sometimes force us to race into our day ill equipped, only to realize later that we need to stop immediately and connect with Jesus if we are going to salvage the day's progress. We can find much to worry about if we allow ourselves. Thoughts and images can capture the mind, massaging them into a panic and sometimes even hysteria. As surely as Jesus didn't want Martha to worry about serving dinner, He doesn't want us to worry about threats of terror or the wicked deeds of others. Look what Proverbs 3:25–26 says about such matters: "Don't fear sudden danger or of the ruin of the wicked when it comes, for the LORD will be your confidence and will keep your foot from a snare" (ESV).

When my mind races ahead to worry about tomorrow, I remind myself that my ever-present God will also be in my future. He will keep me then, just as He is keeping me right now. Knowing my tomorrow holds eternity in heaven and my awesome, big, loving God also holds tomorrow keeps me from stressing and striving.

My eternity has already been planned and prepared. Instead of worrying, I rejoice because God is as much in control in these "last days," as He was when He spoke the universe into existence. "If I go away and prepare a place for you, I will come again and take you to myself, so that where I am you may be also" (John 14:3).

∞ ∞ ∞

When you find your day unraveling right before your eyes and can't seem to stop it from coming undone, you may need to take a Mary moment. Quickly isolate yourself, wherever you are, and call out to the Lord. Be still and allow the awareness of His peace and power to dominate your consciousness and circumstances.

Mary moments are the surest way to
redirect a day gone awry.

It's like pressing the reset button. I've found the quickest and most helpful way to address a sinking heart or a downtrodden spirit is to utter expressions of thankfulness to our Lord.

Thank You that I am never alone.

Thank You for never leaving or forsaking me.

Thank You for your presence and constant companionship.

Thank You for being for me. And if you are for me, who can be against me?

Thank You for giving me the desires of my heart.

Thank You for completing what You have started in me.

Thank You for the desire to do Your good pleasure.

Thank You for working in and through me.

Thank You that Your desire for my life is also my desire for my life.

Thank You that You are the only one I need to please.

Thank You that You are the only one I desire to please.

Thank You that no weapon formed against me will prosper.

Thank You for being my guide and light.

Thank You for showing me the way.

Thank You for making a way for me.

Thank You for going to prepare a place for me.

I guarantee you, you will feel a shift in your spirit after this exercise in gratitude. When I turn my focus to God, my omnipresent Companion, I must acknowledge that He is there all the time.

Sometimes my Mary mornings are merry and my quiet times are not so quiet! The experience makes me wonder why people refer to communication with Jesus as "quiet time." Making a joyful noise unto the Lord, giving Him praises, and demonstrating gratitude can be anything but quiet. I've found that when I start my day with a merry, Mary morning, I am more likely to have expressions of praise continually streaming out of me throughout the day. I feel inoculated against trouble. Please notice; I didn't say I had no challenges. Praising God before trouble appears on our street is like taking a "positive pill." We can handle it a lot better when it eventually arrives. Expressing our gratitude to God is the best way to start any and every day. Doing so immediately shifts our attitudes from being problem focused to being appreciative to God and therefore focused on God. When you are expressing thankfulness, your heart and mind will automatically start pulling your thoughts toward God's goodness, making it the ideal set up for a merry Mary day!

MARTHA-MARY REFLECTIONS

Read and meditate on Matthew 11:29–30 and Romans 8:28. Now reflect on the questions below.

1. If you have a Mary personality, what are some ways you've cultivated your quiet time?

2. If you don't already have a designated quiet time, when will you make yourself available to learn His way and His Word?

3. What steps will you take to stick to your quiet time when it seems difficult?

4. Are you willing to take the time to begin memorizing Scripture verses to empower your life? If yes, when will you get started, and what method will you use.

5. Write some of your own affirmations that will help shift your attitude and perspective when you are having a bad day.

7

A BALANCED MARTHA DAY

∞ ∞ ∞

A balanced Martha day begins with a Mary morning and continues into a day of joyful service unto the Lord. It is a day when you are in continual communion with the Lord. You are open to dialogue about the day's activities but also to change your agenda if you're prompted to do so. As born-again believers, our roles are to be expressions of the love of Jesus in the world. Each day presents its individual set of problems. Responding to them under the direction of the Holy Spirit makes an otherwise messy day, a balanced Martha day. The key to it all is awareness of the presence of God and, through His eyes, the awareness of others' needs. A Mary morning increases your sensitivity in both areas. The discipline of a Mary morning helps us remain focused throughout the day on Jesus Christ and usher in His desires through us. We begin to see the world in an entirely different light. We take note of things we have never noticed before and may even be moved by the Spirit to take action or abandon our agenda completely.

As beloved and chosen children of God, we are on unique

We should be willing to give up our plans
in exchange for God's plans.

---

paths along with other beloved children of God. The Master Planner orchestrates His children and how their lives should intertwine. As our Lord escorts each of us, I pray you enjoy the friends and family He has chosen to experience with you as He prospers you. "We know that all things work together for good of those who love God, who are the called according to his purpose" (Rom. 8:28).

What pleasure it is to seek to please Christ alone. Many Martha types fall into the snare of people pleasing. The more we enjoy knowing His will, the less we care about any perceived expectations of others.

Jesus says, in Matthew 11:29–30: "Take up my yoke and learn from me, because I am lowly and humble in heart, and you will find rest for your souls. For my yoke is easy and my burden is light." Jesus already knows what we are capable of doing, as well as the talents He has given us, which makes Him easy please.

Life, from the perspective of some, can often seem like work, work, and more work. But when we view life from Jesus's perspective, our hearts are made glad by the privilege to serve others on His behalf. As a Martha, it is of utmost importance that I keep this proper perspective, to keep the proper attitude. My earthly father, who is an incredible person and servant of God, frequently says, "People are not using me. God is using me."

When you allow God to use you,
you can't be used by people.

This perspective empowers you to serve with a joyful heart. Recognizing this commission as a higher calling makes for a balanced Martha heart.

Just the thought of having an adventure-filled day makes me feel like an excited child the morning of a school field trip. If this feeling is at all attractive to you, allow me to tell you the quickest way to achieve it. Give your day back to God. Yes, that's right. Give the day God gave you in the first place right back to Him. Now before you panic, Martha, let me just say that God already has your day completely planned. He is well aware of the things you need to get done. If they are genuinely a must, then they are in His plan. You can be assured of that. The major difference between your day and His is that His plan probably has more fun and joy included. So go ahead. You can trust Him. Hand your next twenty-four hours back to Him.

Marthas tend to favor predictability over adventure. Knowing what's next (and then what comes after that) keeps the day moving forward for task-oriented people. After all, getting that mental to-do list completely checked off is the objective of the day, right? Don't we have to have evidence to show how we spent the day? As I searched for the origin of this rigidness, I could trace it

When we go through life with our to-do list always plastered on our windshield and our only objective is to move the items to the done list on the rear glass, we miss out on what God might want to accomplish through us day to day.

back to my developmental years when all my chores had to be completed before I could do the fun stuff. Naturally I've carried this discipline into my adulthood. This discipline obviously has its worth, particularly to an employer or other taskmasters.

When we go through life with our to-do list always plastered on our windshield and our only objective is to move the items to the done list on the rear glass, we miss out on what God might want to accomplish *through* us day to day. Leaving room in your day for adventure might sound a bit ambitious for a true Martha. Let me encourage you to look up. Be available to God as you go about your day. You may be amazed as you become aware of others' needs. The Holy Spirit could prompt you to address others who are on the same path you're traveling. Let the Holy Spirit invade your day. He may ask you to walk by faith. God may request that you step out of your routine to accomplish a greater good than you could have planned. Think of the possibilities!

Expecting God to reveal Himself to me throughout the day is so exciting. I am an individual who has been schedule driven for so many years (and still am, to a lesser degree). Watching for evidence of God in my ordinary day pleasantly adjusts my otherwise project-oriented Martha day to a merry day as well. When I train my thoughts to focus on Jesus Christ living inside me, my whole outlook on life changes. Joy floods my entire being. I also become aware of the angels that are ministering to me and on my behalf. How wonderful it is to realize what is happening in the spiritual realm, setting me up for a great day! "Are they not all ministering spirits sent out to serve those who are going to inherit salvation?" (Heb. 1:14). You may think it's difficult to stay so focused all day, but it gets increasingly easier when you set your mind and spirit on God first thing in the morning.

When our service to God becomes a distraction (thereby taking our attention away from God), we must take a "Mary pill" first thing in the morning and again as needed throughout the day. Not once on Jesus's multiple visits to Martha, Mary, and Lazarus's home do the Gospels record that Jesus supplied the meal. His point

---

Relinquishing control to the rightful owner, our Lord, requires a conscious effort on our part.

---

was not to have Martha discontinue sharing her gift of service and hospitality with Him and the disciples. It was to get her to relinquish that which caused her to be distracted from spending time with Him. I'm convinced this reprimand from the Master caused Martha to restructure her days to be more balanced with a lot less control. People who cherish being in control know exactly where and when they will begin to unravel. We realize when we have taken on too much and are in over our heads.

Once the act of trying to control my surroundings is pried out of my hands, I must admit I am indeed relieved to be out from under the pressure of making sure everything and everyone in my little universe is adequately cared for. If I skip my devotion time, I can easily slip back into the control position. A feeling of being overwhelmed is the first sign that I've overreached and am again weighed down with things God didn't intend for me to carry. For a Martha, having no plan can feel scary and even a bit irresponsible. But knowing that God's plan is the best plan causes me to seek Him for reassurance.

What a privilege to hear from God, know His plan, and be empowered by Him to execute it! Amid this process I can admit I don't know everything (and certainly not the future), but with Jesus living in me, granting me wisdom, and giving me guidance, I don't have to know all the answers because I'm not in my situation alone. I can depend on Him for help in all my circumstances. "Don't worry about anything, but in everything, through prayer and petition with thanksgiving, present your requests to God" (Phil. 4:6).

On certain days, I look at all I have before me and wonder how I'm going to get it all done. Then the Holy Spirit reminds me that the Lord is my strength. I carry on, drawing from His wisdom and knowledge. He is with me. When I take the time to rest in His presence throughout the day, I can feel my worried state rushing away and relaxation arriving. This allows me to experience a fuller measure of God's love for me.

MARTHA-MARY REFLECTIONS

Read and meditate on Philippians 4:6. Then proceed to the following reflection questions.

1. Describe a time when you experienced exhaustion because you were trying to do everything yourself?

2. What challenges your desire to depend totally on Jesus for your physical, emotional, and spiritual needs?

3. What needs to change before you are willing to exchange your "have to do" list for a "blessed to be able to do" list?

4. In what new way(s) are you going to trust God with the details of your agenda?

5. If you are willing to embrace Mary's reality—that she needed Jesus more than anything else—take the time to tell Him right now and resolve to relinquish control of your day-to-day life to Jesus.

8

SUSTAINING PEACE AND STRENGTH

∞ ∞ ∞

My favorite portion of Scripture concerning peace is John 14:27 because it has Jesus describing His gift to us. If God wants us to enjoy one thing while on this earth, it is His peace. Jesus put it this way, "Peace I leave with you. My peace I give to you." I am always amazed that Jesus left us His total peace, not some remnant or residue. He goes on to clarify when He says, "I do not give to you as the world gives. Don't let your heart be troubled or fearful." No, Jesus leaves us His actual, authentically pure, peace. Imagine Jesus taking His calm, contemplative, glorious peace and placing it in you to govern your life. What sweet peace! Few things are as welcoming and as rare as a person who exudes the peace that only the presence of God guarantees.

---

*Having the presence of mind to stay connected
to this ever-present peace is a lifeline that must
be employed daily and exercised continuously.*

Having the presence of mind to stay connected to this ever-present peace is a lifeline that must be employed daily and exercised continuously.

God's presence and the gift of His peace have the ability to stabilize me. Although everything is not perfect, I can enjoy the peace of His presence by allowing it to resonate within me. I don't have to look outside myself for the answers to life's problems; I can look within. The God in me has solutions that help make sense of all my needs. "And the peace of God, which surpasses all understanding, will guard your hearts and minds in Christ Jesus" (Phil. 4:7).

We must closely monitor our stress levels so we don't become someone else's problem. At the first sign of the absence of joy, the question I ask myself is, "What changed"? "You will keep the mind that is dependent on you in perfect peace, for it is trusting in you" (Isa. 26:3).

You may have noticed as soon, as you set your mind to achieve a godly goal or discipline, trouble seemed to find you or distractions tried to derail you. When you think about it, we process thousands of thoughts every day. We make hundreds of decisions, both large and small. Some of our thoughts are fleeting and don't get much attention. Other thoughts are more significant and cause us to pause and ponder them. The chore is to decipher whether the thought is a distraction or an interruption by God.

When that distinction is unclear to you, the Holy Spirit can play an enormous role in your life. Our spirit beings and the Holy Spirit reside in the same room, in the innermost part of our temple. They are in constant dialogue about the matters of the day. Our thoughts are filtered, and then some of them are brought to the spiritual table for discussion. "Don't you know that your body is a temple of the Holy Spirit who is in you, whom you have from God? You are not your own" (1 Cor. 6:19).

My first mental assessment of my thought is a quick one: distraction or instruction? What I'm deciding in real time is the origin of the thought. Is it a distraction from Satan or a reminder/assignment from the sweet Holy Spirit? If it's a distraction, it is quickly exposed, as such, in the light of God's presence. But, if it is the work of the Holy Spirit reminding me of something or giving me an assignment, I quickly acknowledge it. I thank the Holy Spirit for the reminder or the thought. "For although we live in the flesh, we do not wage war according to the flesh, since the weapons of our warfare are not of the flesh, but are powerful through God for the demolition of strongholds. We demolish arguments and every proud thing that is raised up against the knowledge of God, and we take every thought captive to obey Christ" (2 Cor. 10:3–5).

The "mind of my flesh" is inclined to worry about matters that are unimportant. In my life these thoughts usually start with, "what if" or "I wonder." Realizing the vast majority of our "what ifs" never happen, why not quickly discard these thoughts as irrelevant and choose to live in the present reality? If a thought becomes recurring, you must deal with it in the light of God's presence during your quiet time. Submit it to God in prayer and get to the root of its origin. You may discover fear or doubt. You may have a trust issue. You may have a genuine concern, which means it will take more time to process in the presence of God while being aware of His promises.

When you feel yourself losing the "perfect peace" battle, you can regain it immediately with just the mention of His name.

Saying the name Jesus refocuses your attention on Him. Additionally, call on Jesus not only for peace but also for strength. Remember, "the LORD is your strength" (Ps. 28:7). This thought alone is like triggering a relief valve.

Instead of struggling to do something in my strength (and not getting much joy out of it), I remind myself of what Nehemiah 8:10 says, "The joy of the Lord is your strength." An immediate change of attitude and outlook transpires, allowing me to get enjoyment and pleasure out of (almost) any task. Breathe in the peace of His presence and watch your problems diminish. This little exercise helps remind me God is on the throne of my life. I refuse to let my circumstances or problems dethrone Him. "God *is* our refuge and strength, a helper who is always found in times of trouble" (Ps. 46:1).

God is sovereign. He doesn't just offer us insight; He is Lord over *all*—bringing oversight to every situation and circumstance. Count it a privilege to be able to collaborate with the sovereign Lord of the universe. Sometimes the Holy Spirit drops a "God idea" into our spirits. In those instances we should allow ample time for this major interruption. We may need to expound on the thought. It's also a good idea to write the idea or thought down in a journal. You will want to recall the instruction from the Lord in detail and even meditate on the information later.

Obviously, I have not exhausted the many ideas of handling our thought life. I'm sure you have and will discover more on your own as your intimacy with our Lord grows. As you sit in the presence of God, enjoy the peace that surpasses all understanding and His unspeakable joy.

MARTHA-MARY REFLECTIONS

Read Matthew 11:28–30 and reflect on the following questions.

1. How are you displaying the peace of Jesus to the world?

2. Describe a time recently, when you clearly saw God as your refuge?

3. Do you generally ask for God's guidance before or after a crisis arises? Why?

4. How will you change your behavior to corporate a proactive, rather than reactive, approach to God's instructions?

5. Where are you in your commitment to engage in God's Word daily?

9

A LIFESTYLE OF DAILY DEVOTIONAL

∞ ∞ ∞

For Martha types like me, I can't think of another discipline that would be more uncomfortable than the devotion lifestyle. And I don't believe I'm alone in this, so let's take a look at both concepts of discipline and of devotion. In a culture where everyone wants everything "my way" and "right away," the word *discipline* has almost become taboo. Furthermore, the practice of self-discipline is vastly becoming a somewhat outdated idea. The word *devotion* in our modern-day culture almost demands a definition too. Indeed, you may need to dust the word off before using it.

Allow me to refresh the linguistic value of these two terms. Doing so will hopefully cause you to reconsider them and prayerfully strive to achieve the discipline of a devotion lifestyle.

Discipline, used as a noun, usually relates to punishment being inflicted on a person. When the word *discipline* is used as a verb ("to bring to a state of order and obedience by training and control," as per dictionary.com), it takes on an air of one getting it together, usually for the betterment of self.

Devotion, on the other hand, means one must have a profound dedication and consecration. Most of us practice dedication, or the act of being dedicated to something or someone, maybe not as profoundly as we should but to some degree. It's easier to understand *consecration* when we use it as a verb—*consecrating*, which is the act of making sacred, setting apart or dedicating to the service of a deity (in this case, the Lord Jesus Christ). Consecration is the notion of dedicating oneself to the training and practice of setting aside the time required that creates self-consecration unto the Lord.

∞ ∞ ∞

Let's explore some of the how-to items and benefits of the discipline of devotional lifestyles. The first component of a quality devotion experience is showing up. Next, create a place for stillness, reading, and meditation on Scripture. Finally, a place for prayer.

Let's address stillness—another phenomenon that is foreign to our modern-day culture. In the biblical context it is about positioning yourself to receive from God. "Be still and know that I *am* God" (Ps. 46:10 KJV). The concept of being still is a huge challenge for most of us. Stillness in our bodies relieves our minds from the mental task of giving commands and ensuing interaction. We are consciously giving ourselves permission to think of nothing. It is best achieved by just closing our eyes to shut out all visible intrusions from the outside world. The same applies to our ear gate. Shut out all possible noise. Once all is still, we will be able to communicate with God on a spiritual level. In 1 Kings 19:11–13, God spoke to Elijah in "a soft whisper."

God speaks to us in various ways, but the most common avenues are through His Word and through prayer. Holy Scripture is, "inspired by God, and is profitable for teaching, for rebuking, for correcting, for training in righteousness, so that the man of God may be complete, equipped for every good work" (2 Tim. 3:16–17). This verse leaves no doubt about the importance of Scripture. God knew humankind would need instruction for all time. The word of God trains us and teaches us to grow in grace.

The experience of reading the words and thoughts of God as He interacts with human beings is like being tutored by the Holy Spirit.

There is no other place to gain this life-changing knowledge than from the Bible. Do whatever you have to do to foster this discipline. Don't let Satan shortchange you by accepting any of the many excuses he is sure to offer you. When our lives lack godly instruction and training, before long we may find ourselves out of sorts about any and everything. When we gain God's truths, learn more about His character and His unfailing love, we increase in the confidence and strength we need to walk forth more boldly for Him. These Mary moments, early in the morning, are sure to set you up for a great Martha day.

Spending time reading the Word of God is never a futile task or an empty experience. It is the living Word, and it has the power to transform any life that is willing to engage with Scripture. To invest fully we must acknowledge and reverence the Word as truth. We must allow it to renew our thinking, particularly when our thoughts do not agree with God's ageless principles and truths. "Do not be conformed to the age, but be transformed by the renewing of your mind, so that you may discern what is the good, pleasing, and perfect, will of God" (Rom. 12:2).

∞ ∞ ∞

Our next point is the importance of meditating on Scripture. Renewing the mind requires meditating on Scripture that is contrary to our thinking. When the mind is trained a certain way, (and the flesh enjoys the liberty of this particular type of thinking), we may often have to roll God's concept over and over in our mind. It also helps to speak those truths out of our mouth. Verbalizing retrains our thought processes to accept the Word as truth. We may have to repeat these multiple times, depending on how deeply our past erroneous beliefs are rooted. Don't try to rush the process.

Allow the Holy Spirit to help.

He is waiting for you to ask and receive
His instructions.

About ten years ago I participated in a *MasterLife Bible Study*, written by Avery T. Willis Jr., where he instructed us to answer two questions after reading a verse or brief passage of Scripture: "What did God said to me?" and "What have I said to God?" This discipline of reading the passage through a couple of times and then reading it again with the intention of hearing what God is saying and then writing a record of what God said is a wonderful way to encounter Scripture and begin hearing the voice of God through His Word. Once that's done, internalize what God is saying to you and really take it in as the Holy Spirit communicates directly with you. Allow this teaching, direction, and correction to permeate your thinking and then evaluate what you need to adjust, change, or embrace, journaling the new conviction back to God. You will be amazed by the spiritual growth you will experience by just adding this one discipline. After exercising this practice for a while, it will become second nature anytime you read Scripture, making your private time with God all the richer.

Prayer on the other hand requires another level of focus and intentionally. We must stand in faith and awareness that God is listening, that He indeed hears us and cares about our situations.

Prayer is a pouring out of one's heart in
worship and thanksgiving, as well the
submission of petitions for yourself and others.

The Bible tells us God knows what we need before we ask Him, but He still wants us to acknowledge our love and need for Him.

When I was a young girl, we used to sing a song with these lyrics: "Prayer is the key to the kingdom. Faith unlocks the door." Prayer travels straight into the throne room of the Most High God. I love 1 John 5:14, which says, "This is the confidence we have before him: If we ask anything according to his will, he hears us." I often hear people express their frustration about a particular situation by saying, "I've tried everything! The only thing left to do is pray." I'm not sure why we sometimes think of prayer as a last resort.

As children of a loving God, prayer should be
our first instinct when trouble arises.

It is our most powerful weapon. Prayer should be used against the enemy and anything that comes against God's will for our lives and those we love.

Here is your chance to tell the Lord what you need and ask Him to meet your needs. You don't have to ask as if He is unaware of your needs, but ask as a child who comes to a loving father with a request, knowing full well that your Father wants to supply your every need and He is capable of doing so. I've found that when I take my request to the Lord in the morning while I'm calm and at peace, my request is less frantic than if I ask when I've become frustrated with my day. I can ask out of need and desire, not out of frustration. I'm not in a panic with an immediate need; rather I want to wait patiently on God's providential timing.

Prayer connects us with God in a way nothing else can. Something unique about the posture of prayer invites us to open up in total honesty before our loving Father. This welcoming atmosphere urges us to unload the burdens we've been trying to carry alone. When we ask and receive from the only true Help, we can know that He is listening, and we can rest assured that He will answer. "Because he has his heart set on me, I will deliver him; I will protect him, because he knows my name. When he calls out to me, I will answer him; I will be with him in trouble. I will rescue him and give him honor" (Ps. 91:14–15).

I have difficulty conceiving that anyone would opt out of talking to God if given the chance, but people do it all the time. They apparently do not fully understand this supernatural process and accumulate a countless number of missed opportunities to include God in their lives. Perhaps it's because we don't always physically see God at work. Most of His work is done behind the scenes. But concluding that prayer is a waste of time or the last resort is false and erronus.

Lastly, like all conversations, prayer should be a two-way conversation. Once you have stated your request, sit still awhile and listen for what God may have to say to you. You won't always hear

His small voice, but pause long enough to let Him respond, remembering He speaks to the heart. This is communing with God!

MARTHA-MARY REFLECTIONS

Read Psalm 91:14–15. Then reflect on the questions below.

1. What are some new ways you can make talking with God in prayer more enjoyable?

2. Understanding the value of God's Word, what steps are you willing to take to engage more in Scripture?

3. Give two reasons why you feel that meditating on Scripture is beneficial?

4. What are two questions you can ask yourself to help you connect with God in a more meaningful way?

5. **What specific part of your day will you spend getting to know God intimately?**

IO

REST ASSURED

∞ ∞ ∞

How does a Martha master sitting still in her Mary morning? Especially while all of the day's worries are on her mind and beckoning for immediate attention? Well, let me tell you how this Martha handles her morning when the day wants to race ahead of me. *Stop, drop, and roll.* First, I *stop* my mind from racing out of control. I *stop* and acknowledge God and the fact that He is in control. He has a perfect plan for my day. Then, I *drop* the notion that I know what's best. I *drop* my agenda in exchange for the perfect day He had planned for me before He formed me. I *drop* to my knees yielded and willing to carry out His plan. Finally, I *roll* my cares onto Him, knowing He cares for me. Now, with a much lighter load or maybe even no load at all, I can carry on throughout my day, seeking Him and recognizing His hand in the details. This prescription causes me to be the best Martha I can be. I'm then the Martha He created me to be, enjoying the rest He encourages me to enter.

Rest is another word that doesn't seem to receive much attention by today's restless generation—at least not in the general sense of the word, and certainly not in the ideal sense of what rest entails. Rest, in both aspects, requires us to put our load down both physically and mentally. Much of our anxiety comes from our inability to do just that. We want to carry our burdens and agonize over how to fix them, which is exactly the opposite of how Jesus wants us to respond to the stresses of life.

Jesus wants us to bring our burdens to Him
and let Him carry them.

He wants to work out the solution for us. "Cast your burden on the LORD, and he will sustain you; he will never allow the righteous to be shaken" (Ps. 55:22).

One of the mottos I used to subscribe to was, "Putting it on my calendar takes it off my mind." I must admit it is a Martha motto. There is nothing spiritual about it at all, but it worked for a while. But when I began having Mary mornings, I realized that not carrying any load at all was even better. A load can constitute many things: a project, a person, a problem, or even something from a to-do list.

What could be better than putting it all at Jesus's feet? When I peer to the coming days ahead, I realize my deficiencies. I must be honest and admit I am inadequate to sustain myself even on this day.

Do not fear, for I am with you; do not be afraid, for I am your

I am reassured by the thought that the same loving and able God, who is keeping me today, will also be the same willing and able Sustainer tomorrow.

God. I will strengthen you; I will help you; I will hold you with my righteous right hand" (Isa. 41:10). Who wouldn't want to take hold of these promises before embarking on their day? Who can handle each problem and circumstance without Him?

∞ ∞ ∞

How awesome it is to rest in the presence of the Lord and let His Holy Spirit minister to our needs. Just being reassured of His companionship and guidance is liberating. The ability to reveal and relinquish all worries, doubts, and fears releases us from any power they may have over us. After we've received this ministry from God, we should have a different perspective and a new outlook on our situations.

As I sit and enjoy my Mary morning, after being in the presence of my Lord and all that His presence offers, I'm reminded and assured that this act of devotion will never be taken away from me. My heart leaps for joy and flutters with expectation at the thought of my ongoing relationship with God getting richer and stronger day by day and year after year. All of a sudden growing old doesn't seem scary at all. Loneliness will never be a part of my future.

Allow the Lord's presence to chase away all anxiety, strife, and chaos from your being. Allow Him to replace it with a quiet resolve that all things (mentally, physically, and spiritually) will be available, as needed, in sufficient proportions. Rest! Why try to carry all you think you will need for every part of your journey? God wants you to hold His hand and trust Him to provide. We have two choices: we can carry the overweight backpack up the mountain straining and tiring under its load. Or we can hold God's steady hand

You will never be alone.

The forever, all-knowing, all-sufficient Lord
your God is ever present on the scene.

up the mountain, relying on Him to provide the necessities along the way. Recognize you are not alone.

Let's focus briefly again on meditating on Scripture. Unfortunately meditation is sometimes misunderstood in the Christian community. Permit me to clarify. We are *not* meditating to keep thoughts out of our mind. We are meditating on Scripture to *renew* our mind in a particular area, which is one of the most intentional things we can do during our quiet times. It is notably effective when fears and worries are the order of the day. Reminding ourselves of the promises God made to His children is the quickest way to calm our fears. This type of meditation reminds us who is in control.

This sacred time should be set aside to get to know God. We want to know Him as a Father and Friend. We desire to know Him as a Savior and Sustainer. We need to know Him as Righteousness and Redeemer. In our time with God, we can discover so many of His descriptive attributes: the good Shepherd, God Almighty, the Lord our Righteousness, our Healer, our Redeemer, the everlasting God.

We will never exhaust all the facets of God!

Discovering each newly revealed level of God brings more adoration and the longing to know Him even more intimately. The experience is like floating down a lazy river, stopping along the way to explore the sights on the riverbank but then hastening to continue because more scenes are available to explore just ahead.

My prayer for you, as you long for more of God, can be found in Ephesians 3:17:19: "That Christ may dwell in your hearts through faith. I pray that you, being rooted and firmly established in love, may be able to comprehend with all the saints what is the length and width, height and depth of God's love, and to know Christ's love that surpasses knowledge, so that you may be filled with all the fullness of God."

The thought so humbles me that the Spirit of the almighty eternal God of the universe desires to dwell in me and live through me during my life span. What an honor to be used by Him to impact the world. Meditate on this for a moment. You can become a valuable change agent for Christ in the world. The first step is to acknowledge the role in which God wants you to engage. Second, we must set aside our agenda to accept this remarkable role.

MARTHA-MARY REFLECTIONS

Read 2 Corinthians 10:5. Then reflect on the questions below.

1. In your own words describe what it means to "rest" in God's presence?

2. How are you going to respond to Jesus's invitation to cast your burdens on Him?

3. In what areas are you seeking God to strengthen you?

4. How are you going to involve God as you navigate your day?

5. What are some things you have done to become more comfortable with being still and getting to know God more deeply?

11

SUMMING IT ALL UP!

∞ ∞ ∞

The gift of God's company and the continuous dialogue we enjoy is indeed a gift and a blessing. After spending years invested in this consecrated time with my Lord, I can't help but feel every second of my life has had His blessing upon it. In a day and age when the common behavior indicates that "time is money," tithing our time (or giving God the firstfruit of our morning) is enormously beneficial. When we allow the Lord to order our steps, we will find it takes fewer steps and less time to accomplish any task or assignment. We have two choices; we can go through life feeling as though time is slipping through our fingers, or we can employ this precious gift of time we've been granted to accomplish what He purposed us to achieve. The latter is one sure way to live a life worthy of the epitaph: "a life well spent."

Many times I know the devotion or Scripture for the day is the exact counseling or reassurance I needed. I have no doubt God is with me. In fact, He is leading me by lighting my path. And I am gladly following.

Jesus wants to fill us with His purpose for the sake of His kingdom but also for our benefit. The benefits of such a daily encounter are both spiritual and physical.

- Our ear is tuned to hear the voice of God.
- We respond to God's voice regularly.
- We become keenly aware that we are never alone.
- We receive clear direction from our Maker.
- We are full of His reassurance along the way.

∞ ∞ ∞

"My sheep hear my voice, I know them, and they follow me" (John 10:27).

∞ ∞ ∞

"You reveal the path of life to me; in your presence is abundant joy; at your right hand are eternal pleasures" (Ps. 16:11).

Seeking the Lord Jesus early in the morning gives us the benefit of a full day of miraculous happenings

Breathe in God's goodness and dispel grappling and greed.

Breathe in His grace and expel grabbing and grasping.

Breathe in God's mercy and minimize others' mistakes.

Breathe in His love and lavish love on everyone we encounter.

My motivation for writing this book was to encourage and inspire Jesus's followers. It is meant for people of all ages, genders and walks of life. I intended to explain the benefits of adopting the habit of spending a specific time alone with God every day.

You may still be asking yourself where you will get the time to be with God every day. It seems like such a luxury. My experience has been that God will honor your sincere desire to have daily quiet time. He will supply both the time and the lifestyle that allow you to cultivate a relationship with Him.

God wants this time with you more than you do.

God didn't make humankind because He needed them. He wants relationships. Still, for any relationship to be mutually satisfying, both sides must do their part.

Remember: "He rewards those who seek him" (Heb. 11:6).

Please allow me to conclude by offering this prayer to recite when things get tough.

∞ ∞ ∞

Dear Lord,

When my faith is failing, may meditating on Your Word usher me into Your presence and bolster my faith. When my peace is waning, may the power of Your Word soothe my frazzled mind and grant me Your peace. When my joy lacks luster, may your renewing Word rejuvenate my spirit, yielding unspeakable joy. Lord, I receive Your faith and welcome Your peace and patience. Please help me extend the same patience to others. I release my problems and concerns into Your Hands. I will walk away with a Mary heart and desire to please You by fulfilling the Martha purpose You have for my day. In Jesus's name, I pray. Amen.

Made in the USA
San Bernardino, CA
21 March 2019